Princess Gabby Girl and the Sparkly Dress

Camille Battaglia

Illustrated by Karen Wolcott

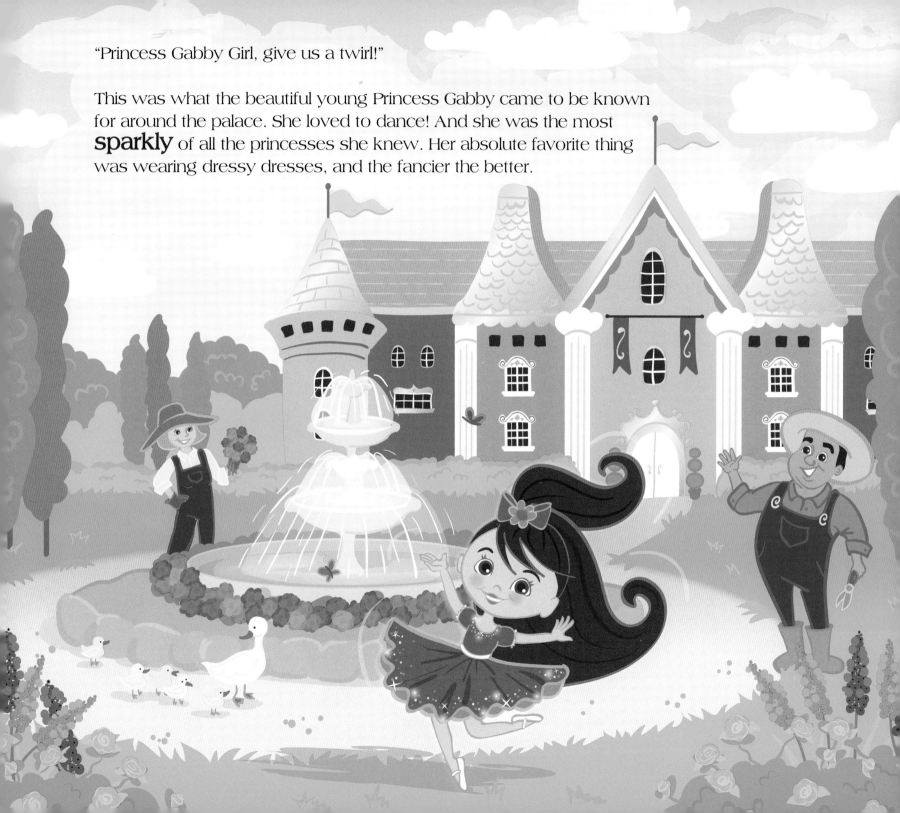

"Princess Gabby Girl, give us a twirl!"

This was what the beautiful young Princess Gabby came to be known for around the palace. She loved to dance! And she was the most **sparkly** of all the princesses she knew. Her absolute favorite thing was wearing dressy dresses, and the fancier the better.

One **sunny** morning, Princess Gabby skipped to her closet and chose a lovely gold, shimmery, twirly dress.

She danced around the palace and her **joy** could be felt by everyone!

She leapt and spun down the longest hallway until she noticed a light twinkling on the wall beside her. The princess followed the light into a room she had never been in before...

...and found a gorgeous, glowing mirrored wardrobe.

The door was open just a crack, and when Princess Gabby looked inside, she gasped in **awe** and **wonder**.

There, hanging in the closet, was the most **extraordinary** dress! It was pink like a sunset in summer, light and soft like a bouquet of baby's breath, and covered from top to bottom in *sparkles*!

Princess Gabby quickly put on the dress. She looked in
the mirror and squealed with delight. She was **radiant**!
"I will never take this dressy dress off, not ever!"

Just then, the mirror trembled and shined so **bright** that the princess had to close her eyes for a moment.

"Hello, Princess Gabby," said a soft, **gentle** voice.

Princess Gabby jumped back. There was a face–pretty like a princess's–inside the mirror! And it was talking to her!

The face in the mirror smiled warmly at Princess Gabby. She was a little startled but realized that the **nice** thing to do was to say hello.

"Um, hello, ah...Mirror..." Princess Gabby began. "It's a pleasure to meet you." She curtsied.

"How very polite indeed," the mirror said. "I am Miss Marvelous, and it's been centuries since a little princess has **loved** the sparkly dress enough to wake me."

Princess Gabby gave a twirl to show just how much she **adored** the dress.

"Now to keep this dress shining brightly, there are two things you must do. One: You must always use **kind words**. And two: You must always do **good deeds**. Can you do that?"

"Yes, Miss Marvelous!" The princess smiled brightly. "**Kindness and good deeds**, always!"

Miss Marvelous quickly disappeared in a burst of light.

Princess Gabby took one more look at her **dazzling** dress
and then rushed off to show it to her family.

"Oh, Princess Gabby, you sparkle like the sun!" said the queen.

"Thank you, Mama!" The princess couldn't wait to see how her dress might shimmer outside. "May I please go to the village park and play?"

"Yes, sweetie, but please take your little brother with you," said the queen.

"Of course!" Princess Gabby clasped her little brother's hand. She had wanted to skip and dance her way there, but she happily slowed down to wait for Prince Chas to toddle along beside her.

When Chas tripped on a cobblestone, Princess Gabby stopped to **kiss** his boo-boo and give him a **hug**.

When they saw a little girl drop her dolly, the princess picked it up and rushed after the girl to return it.

And when Princess Gabby and Prince Chas finally made it to the park in the village, the princess's dress was **shining** even brighter than before!

Princess Gabby spread **love and light** everywhere she went. She sparkled at home, she sparkled in the village, and she sparkled at school.

On the playground at school she **cheered** up her older brother, Prince Paulie, when he didn't do well on a test. She made silly faces until he was **laughing** too.

Princess Gabby made a new friend in Chloe when she **shared** her pretty pink princess cake with her at lunch.

While walking home from school, Princess Gabby noticed one of the palace puppies, named Beau, had wandered off, and she **smiled** as she brought him back to his royal doghouse.

And the princess invited everyone–yes, **everyone**–from school to her dress-up birthday ball at the palace. She even shared all her new toys with them!

Early the morning after her birthday ball, Prince Chas was making an awful racket with his toy bubble-blowing lawn mower in the hallway.

Princess Gabby stumbled out of bed and...stubbed her toe on the nightstand–ouch! When she stood up again, she bonked her head on the edge of her bed–double ouch!

The princess did not feel very sparkly at all.

Still sniffling, Princess Gabby put on her dress and went down to the palace sun room for breakfast. She liked to eat pancakes for breakfast every morning, thank you very much. But this morning the princess had put pepper on her pancakes thinking they were sprinkles. Princess Gabby did *not* like pepper. Pepper was *not* pretty.

The princess was tired. The princess's toe hurt (and her forehead, too!). And now the princess was hungry.

The royal chef asked if Princess Gabby liked her pancakes, and she replied (not very kindly), "No! I do not. Not at all!"

"Sorry, Princess," the royal chef said. "Can I make you something else?"

"No!" replied the princess curtly.

Princess Gabby thought the chef looked a little sad. But Princess Gabby was not going to try even one bite of her pancakes with pepper on top. She didn't bother to tell the chef about her mistake of peppering her pancakes!

After breakfast, when Prince Chas wanted to play with the big, bouncy ball the princess had gotten for her birthday, Princess Gabby gave a firm "No!"

When it was time to go to school, and the queen asked Princess Gabby to put on her glass slippers, Princess Gabby declared, "I am not going to school."

Of course, even princesses must go to school, but Princess Gabby was not happy about it.

After taking a very, very, very, very long time to put on her glass slippers, the princess finally stomped out the door. And, grumpy as she was, she did not realize that her dress was a little less glittery than it had been the day before…

Princess Gabby could not seem to get out of her grouchy mood. It followed her everywhere. By the end of the week, she was saying things like: "I am not taking turns with my friends," and "I am not eating my vegetables," and "I am not helping to clean up."

Slowly her dress was losing its shimmer.

After the princess shouted at her little brother for spilling milk on her dress, the queen said, "Princess Gabby, have you noticed that your dress isn't shining?"

Princess Gabby looked down. Her dress was dingy and dirty. Many of the sparkles were hanging on by a thread and all of them were very dull.

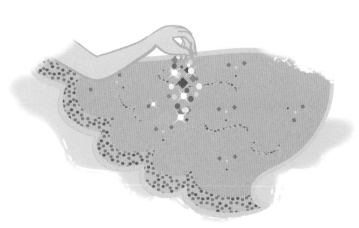

Princess Gabby tried to wash her dress.

She tried to hang her dress in the sun.

She even tried to sprinkle glitter on it.

But nothing made the dress really glow. Finally, out of ideas, Princess Gabby went to put it back in the mirrored closet where she had found it.

Just when Princess Gabby walked into the room, the mirrored closet began to tremble. A bright light beamed, and the princess had to cover her eyes for a moment.

When she opened them, Miss Marvelous was looking at her from the mirror. "Princess Gabby, have you forgotten the secret to your dress shining brightly?"

Princess Gabby nodded and stared down at the dull dress in her hands.

"You must **always be kind** and do **good deeds**," Miss Marvelous said gently. "Without that, you will lose your shine and be very sad indeed."

"I know," said the princess. That was exactly what had happened.

The princess remembered how sparkly she felt when she shared her pretty pink princess cake with Chloe. She remembered how sparkly she felt when she gave the doll back to the little girl. She remembered how sparkly she felt on her birthday when she shared her toys. And she remembered how sparkly she always felt, long before the magic dress, when she played and laughed with Prince Chas and Prince Paulie.

Suddenly the princess shouted, "I get it! When I thought only about me, myself, and I, my dress turned dark. I am so sorry! Sorry to everyone!"

"Yes," said Miss Marvelous. "When you are **giving and kind**, when you share and think of others, you will be **happy**. And then your dress will shine forever." With that, the mirror beamed again, and when Princess Gabby opened her eyes, her dress was radiant!

Princess Gabby put her dress back on. She looked at herself in the mirror and at the light twinkling on the walls around her.

She learned a valuable lesson that day. ...*If you make the light shine in others, it will shine in you, too!*

Once again the princess began to shine all through her house, and all through her school, and all through her village, and all through her country, and all through the world...

You are the light of the world–like a city on a hilltop that cannot be hidden.
No one lights a lamp and then puts it under a basket.
Instead, a lamp is placed on a stand,
where it gives light to everyone in the house.
In the same way, let your good deeds shine out for all to see,
so that everyone will praise your heavenly Father.

(Matthew 5:14-16)

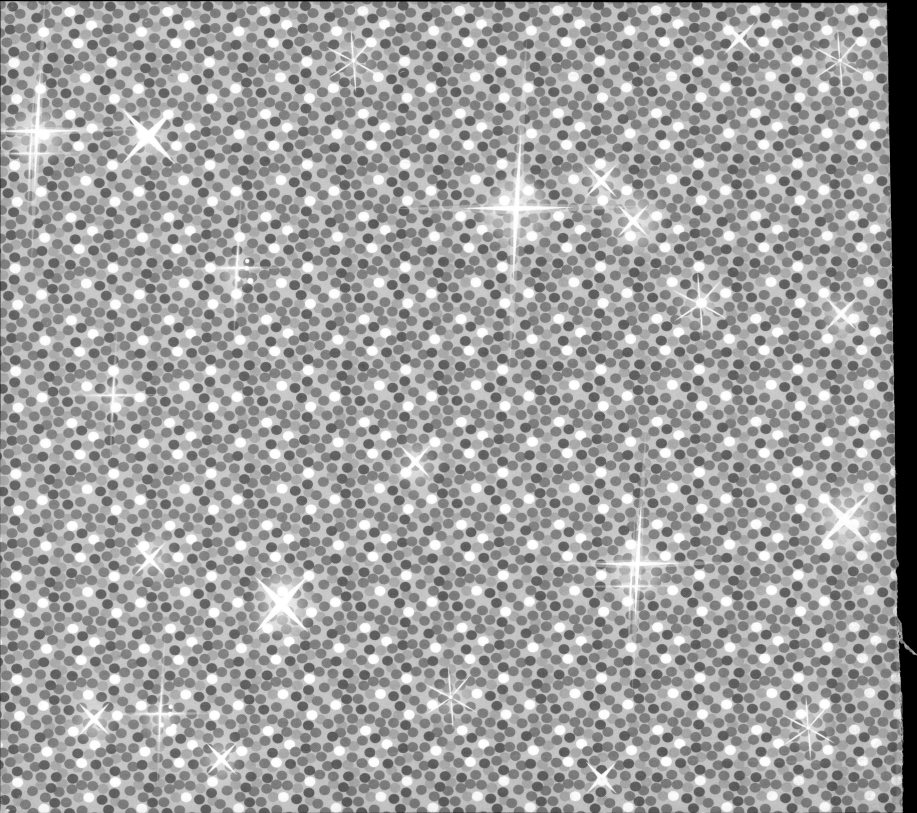